Corfu Donkey Rescue

Waltraud Lederer

Corfu Donkey Rescue

New home for abandoned and old donkeys

Bibliografische Information der Deutschen Nationalbibliothek:
Die Deutsche Nationalbibliothek verzeichnet diese Publikation in der
Deutschen Nationalbibliografie; detaillierte bibliografische Daten
sind im Internet über http://dnb.dnb.de abrufbar.

Illustration: Waltraud Lederer

Herstellung und Verlag: BoD – Books on Demand, Norderstedt
ISBN: 978-3-7357-5960-3

For Judy Quinn
who started this unique project

Thank you Judy

Preface

I have written this book with the intention to encourage all animal lovers to participate as a volunteer in this project. It is not as complicated as it may appear. Applying for this job and organizing it is absolutely easy with Corfu Donkey Rescue (CDR).

I would like to talk about my tasks at CDR and the experiences I made on the following pages.

First of all, I am going to describe the characteristics of a typical Corfu donkey and the aims of CDR.

Waltraud Lederer

Why Corfiot donkeys are living in conditions of great misery

Corfiot donkeys have mainly been used for transporting people or working hard seasonally as pack animals for the olive harvest. The donkeys' situation has worsened due to their small size, the fact that human beings do not know enough about the needs, the proper feed and the medical care of the animals. The design of the Corfiot saddle called Samara is so bad that even young donkeys suffer from permanent health damages.

Due to growing technologization agriculture and the donkey being used as a "workhorse" lost more and more significance, not only in Corfu, but all over Greece. The donkeys' owners have appreciated them less and less, they have degraded them as animals for slaughter to be transported to Italian slaughterhouses. Nobody has cared about their well-being during these transports.

The main task of Corfu Donkey Rescue during the past years has been to avoid these transports by housing old, injured or ill donkeys in the donkey shelter. CDR's maxim is that donkeys deserve a happy and species-appropriate evening of life after having worked for a period of approximately 20 years.

The burden carried by a donkey should not exceed 20 % of his own weight including the net weight of the packsaddle.

Otherwise permanent health damages of the donkey would be the consequence.

What Corfu Donkey Rescue is aiming at

CDR was founded in 2004 by the Englishwoman Judy Quinn who has been living on this island for several years. The rescue station wants that

- old donkeys have a safe and happy evening of life
- sick donkeys are cured
- injured donkeys recover from their injuries
- abandoned donkeys get a feeling of security again
- all donkeys have a better life.

As a result of CDR's support, the transports from Corfu to Italian slaughterhouses could effectively be stopped.

However, CDR's success depends on the help of volunteers.

Students studying animal health are always welcome to do an internship and volunteers supporting CDR are welcome throughout the year.

An evening of life spent with fellow members of the species without any fears and sorrows

There is enough food for all donkeys

A safe and comfortable stable for spending the night

Sheltered in summer as well as in winter

All about me

My name is Waltraud Lederer. I am a Bachelor Professional (CCI) of Business and I am working in the financial controlling department of a Bavarian company. Bavaria is a beautiful place to live.

I have a great passion for donkeys and I love participating in donkey trekkings since there is nothing more beautiful for me but exploring nature together with a donkey.

In August 2012 I had worked as a volunteer in the donkeys' stable of an animal sanctuary in Austria for two weeks. Since then I cannot imagine living without these lovable creatures any longer. Akis, the female donkey I am supporting with financial means now, had adopted me (not the other way round ☺) during these two weeks. Since that time I have been working every 4th Saturday in Akis' sanctuary.

On Easter Sunday in 2008, Akis, a Greek donkey, had been sent to Austria together with a group of donkeys by CDR. Last year I wanted to know more about Akis' former home and her origin and I googled CDR in the Internet. I was really moved by the statements on the website: Judy Quinn, a British citizen, had founded a sanctuary for donkeys in Greece!

It is not easy to establish a sanctuary for animals in Germany, but in Southern countries you are encountered with many more difficulties. Animal protection in Greece does not have the same significance as in Germany. A donkey is merely considered as a "workhorse" there.

Do you know that donkeys can smile? No? Akis has a beautiful smile!

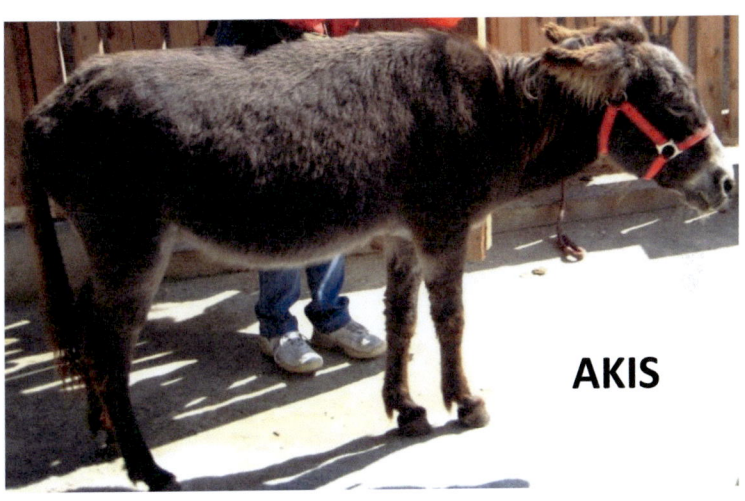

AKIS

Working at CDR without any bureaucratic burdens

Under the heading "volunteering" of the quadrilingual CDR homepage (German, English, Netherland and Greek) all necessary information is given.

It is not assumed that you already have had any contact with donkeys; however, the will to learn and put a jerk in it is essential. Only English is spoken in the donkey shelter, this is why you should be able to speak this language.

These are the daily chores:

- Feeding the animals
- Watering the animals
- Cleaning the stables and the area around the stables
- Routine work for donkeys, dogs and cats
- Brushing/grooming
- Occupying your time with the donkeys
- Going for a walk with a donkey
- Guiding visitors

In the hospital/treatment stable students and trainees are instructed in first aid measures and the daily basic chores for the animals. Volunteers who are interested in this work are also welcome to inform as many people as possible on the donkeys' needs in return.

Information on direct flights to Corfu, the distance between the airport and CDR and the description of how to get there can be found on the CDR website under the heading "volunteering".

CDR has agreed on special prices with the pension "The Achilleas" for volunteers and students. A single-bed room including a shower, a toilet, a TV set and the joint use of a common kitchen costs only 70 € a week, a double-bed room costs 105 €. CDR will book the room in the name of the volunteer. More comfortable hotel rooms can be rented at reduced prices.

CDR has agreed upon fixed terms with a taxi company for drives to and from the airport. You only have to send an SMS the day before arriving in Corfu, refer to CDR, inform on the time of arrival and the flight number and you will be awaited at the airport by a person showing a name tag.

„Pension The Achilleas"

Although the pension is situated in the vicinity of the donkey shelter, CDR will assist you renting a motor scooter or a bicycle at reduced prices. So volunteers can get to know the beautiful landscape nearby. Moreover, in a local taverna you can enjoy excellent meal at reduced prices.

As soon as you have decided to support CDR by working with them, you only have to download the form for "volunteers" or for "students", fill it in and send it back. This is all you have to do for the moment.

In case you have any questions, just write an e-mail to CDR and you will get a friendly answer.

Taverna Elizabeth – reduced prices for CDR students and volunteers

Exploring the beautiful landscape during leisure time

What are the next steps?

CDR sent me a confirmation and told me that they were looking forward to meeting me. They sent me a short description of a typical working day with the donkeys.

Actually, I have not been a fan of Facebook, however, I found two open groups of Corfu Donkey Rescue - a German and an International one. In the first two weeks, I was only reading the statements of Facebook users since here a lot of information on actual developments at CDR could be found. Within these two weeks I noted a high degree of harmony and team spirit among the users writing their statements and comments and I was glad to join the group.

The fact that all members of the group are interested in the well-being of donkeys and that all of them intend to help makes the group so attractive. For example, a woman working at CDR informed us that a certain medicine was not available in Greece and asked if somebody could donate one package. A group member who frequently visits CDR informed the others that the package could be sent to her, she would take it with her, thus saving forwarding costs abroad. This is how group members help each other.

Many people have chosen a donkey at CDR that they support financially. Facebook offers the chance to see the latest photos and get the latest information.

Other members do handicrafts and offer their products on a virtual flea market, the profit will be sent to CDR.

The team spirit of the friends of CDR

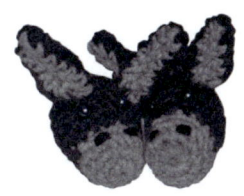

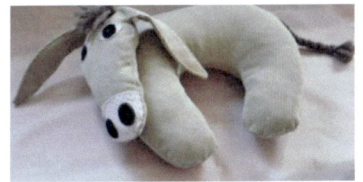

A selection of attractive products made by the friends of CDR - the profit is sent to CDR

Regularly news is sent from the donkey shelter, such as a message from Judy: "This is our new donkey Amalia ..."

Some members of the Facebook group have already been with CDR and all of them have been talking enthusiastically on this stay: Whoever has been there will return again and again.

I informed the group on my plans to work at CDR as a volunteer for a period of two weeks. The members of the group shared my pleasant anticipation and I got a lot of positive resonance.

My excitation was growing with the departure date coming nearer and nearer. The reason was not because I did not know what laid ahead, the reverse was true. I was looking forward to that stay very intensely. I wanted to share this feeling of joy with the other members of the group and posted a picture I had drawn myself showing how I imagined this journey to look like.

Finally, on 24 May 2014 the day had come, I flew to Corfu and

Corfu Donkey Rescue.

Working as a volunteer for the welfare of animals for two weeks! On the following pages I would like to show you how much I enjoyed the stay and which tasks I had to do.

Koffer voller Streichel-
einheiten für: Mithi
claudi Cookie
Morgan Ziggy Aria siε
Aris Mandou Anzio Siren
Anidola Dina Christos
Sorali: Hansel
Iraklis Circa Harvey
und viele mehr ...

Grüße der
ausgewanderten
griechischen Esel
Aki's, Etsi, Silla,
Kiriaki, Mouse
und Batis

Ticket Corfu

CDR
Corfu
Donkey
Rescue

Aris Ball

Finally arrived!

The morning routine starts with the most important task

Elderly donkeys or handicapped donkeys cannot get up on their own. They can be assisted by two persons drawing a blanket under the belly and lifting it simultaneously at the right and at the left. Depending on its constitution, the donkey will try to stand up. In case of very weak animals, the donkey is helped by four persons.

When the donkey stands on his feet, he is supported by the blanket until he safely stands on his feet. In most cases, the donkey can walk around without any problems all day long.

It is important that this procedure is done first at the very beginning of the day, for otherwise the donkey will constantly try to get up on his own, thus wearing off his skin. This routine provides safety and confidence to the donkey, so that he can wait patiently for help.

This task is given top priority by CDR. Every day we had helped the donkeys first, afterwards everybody could fulfil the other tasks assigned to him/her.

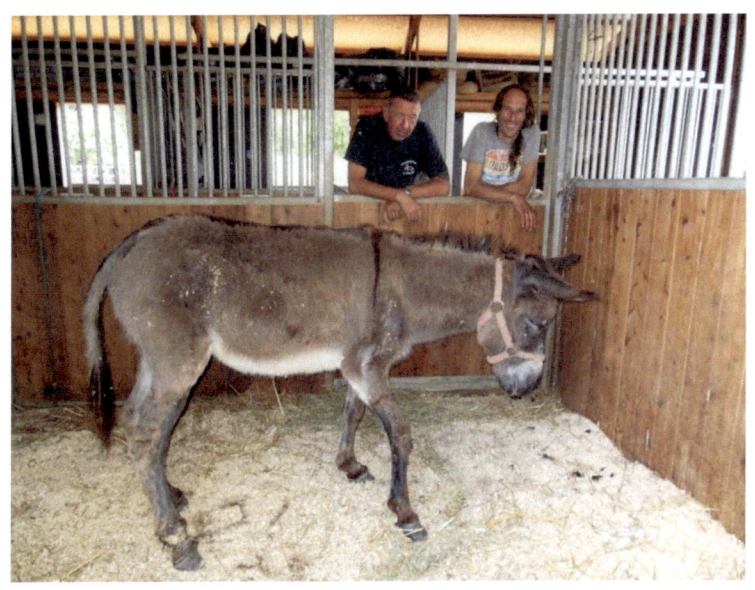

A donkey unable to get up on his own was supported by these helpers.

Feeding

Feeding starts at 9 o'clock in the morning and at 4 o'clock in the afternoon. There is a feeding plan for every donkey according to which the animal care worker mixes the fodder and adds some medicine, if necessary. Before starting feeding, the donkeys are leashed to ropes that had been distributed all over the area so that every donkey gets the fodder and medicine according to the feeding plan. The donkeys seem to know the feeding time and are loitering around the ropes waiting to get fed.

Only after every donkey has emptied his feeding trough, the ropes are removed again. If one of the donkeys does not empty his trough, an animal care worker is informed and shown the rest of the fodder. Donkeys suffer without mourning in case of illness. If a donkey does not eat all the fodder, this can be seen as hint as to his physical condition.

As soon as the ropes have been removed from the donkeys, Trifili (a mixture of hay and grass) is distributed in a pushcart. First it is put into big containers, then it is distributed in small heaps all over the area, so that every donkey can find a place and no jealousy about food can develop.

Fodder and medicine according to the feeding plan for all donkeys.

Donkeys waiting for Trifili.

Cleaning the feeding troughs and filling the water troughs

After feeding the donkeys, all feeding troughs are cleaned by removing rests of fodder and potential contaminations with a brush.

Big water troughs are provided for the animals at several spots on the area. The water troughs are emptied, cleaned and filled up again with a hose. Also the water buckets in the stable boxes are emptied, cleaned and filled again.

Cleaning the fodder troughs.

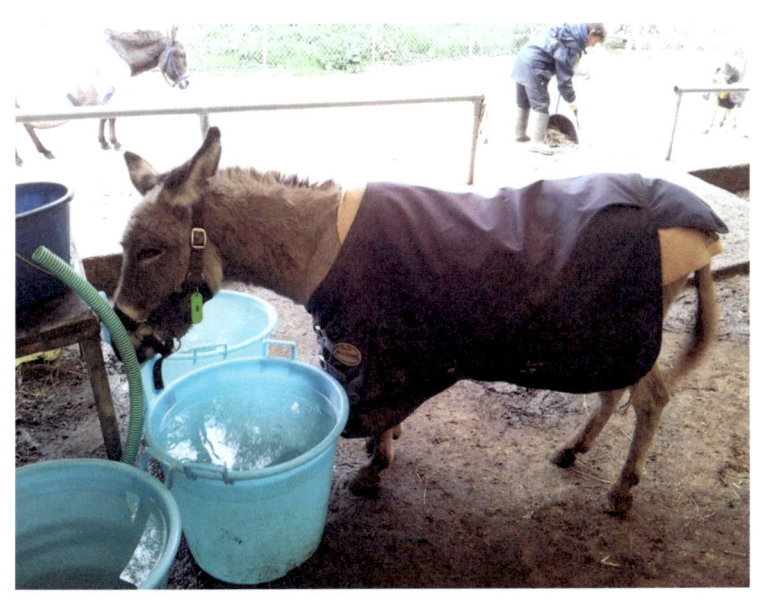

Water troughs have been filled with fresh water

Wound treatment

Many injured donkeys come here. It may take a long time until the wounds have been cured. Wound treatment is done by animal care workers of CDR or medical students. The dressings are changed. Volunteers being interested get explanations and the opportunity to assist the animal care workers.

The donkeys get "trousers" that keep flies away from the dressings.

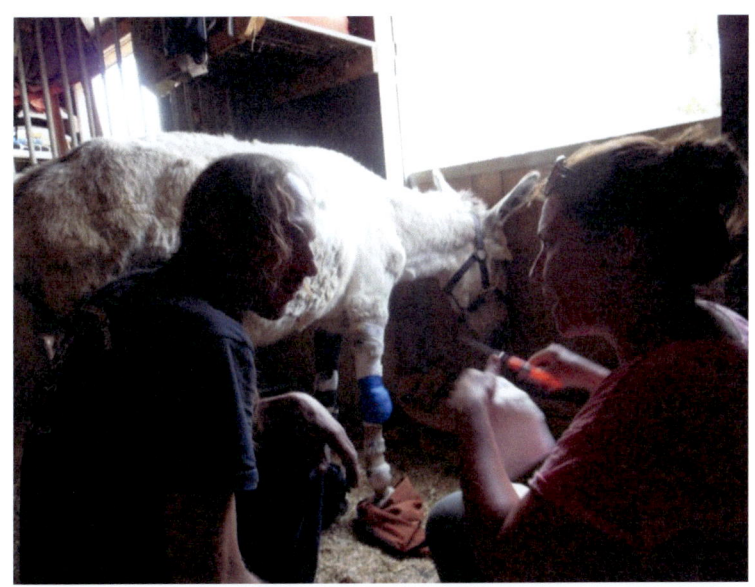

Changing the dressings.

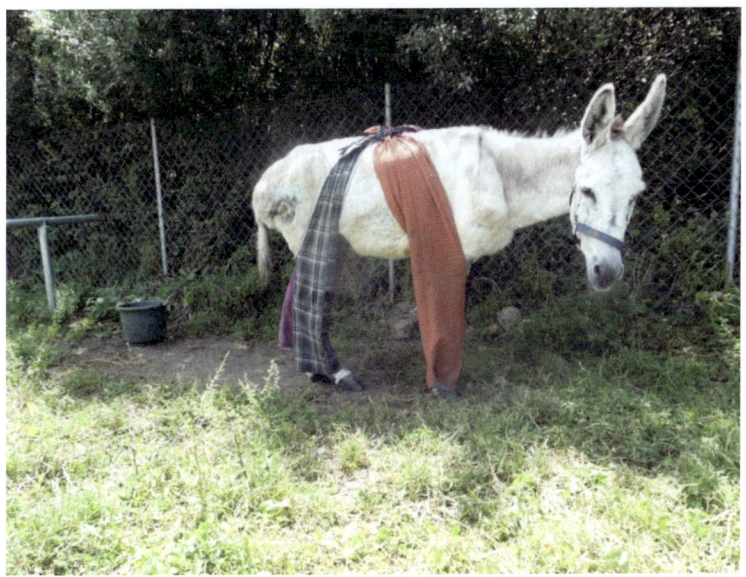

The dressings are covered by protective "trousers".

Examination of newly arrived donkeys

Newly arrived donkeys are thoroughly examined as to injuries and/or evidences of disease. Then a fodder and treatment plan is made.

Arrival of a new donkey - controlling the hooves

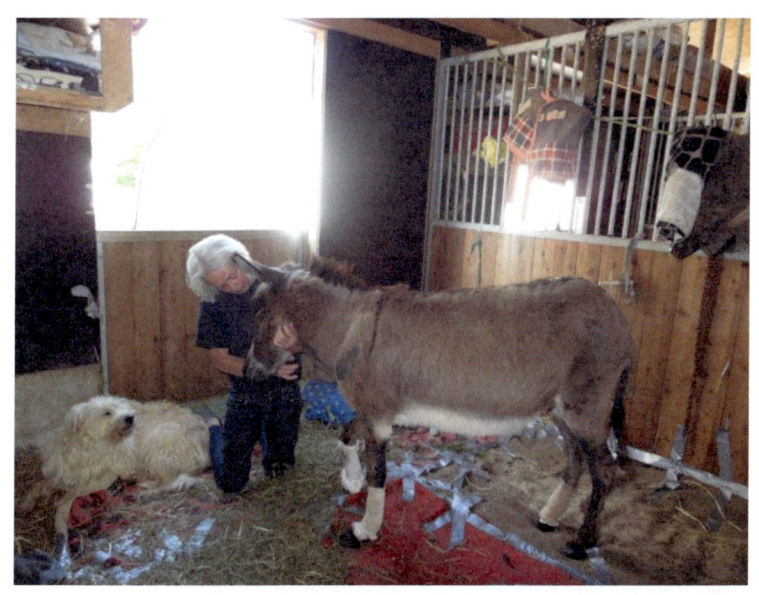

Health check of a donkey after having arrived at CDR

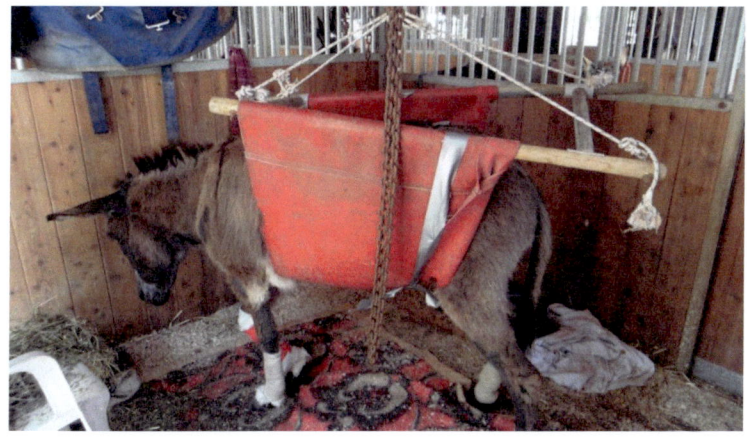

The injured donkey gets a standing aid for being able to breathe
more easily in an upright position

Cleaning out the stables

Here a lot must be done. Every day the treatment stables, the big tent for donkeys, the stables of the blind donkeys and the boxes for the horses are thoroughly cleaned out.

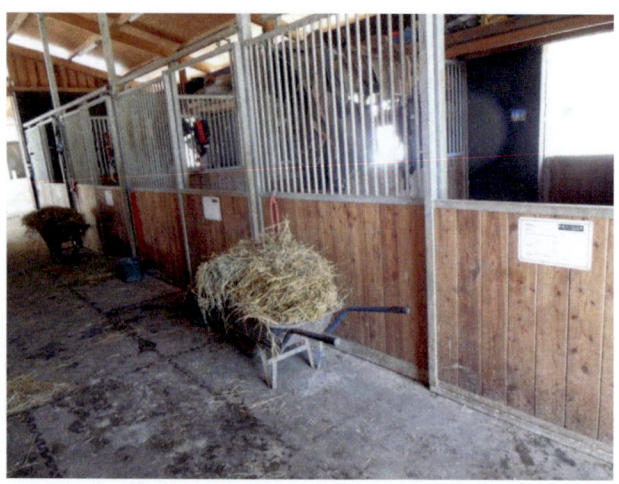

Picking up donkey droppings and dog dirt

Donkey droppings are removed every day. Animal care workers go over the area with a sack truck for picking up the donkey droppings with a moulded manure scoop. The donkey droppings are stored in textile sacks. Farmers appreciate the high quality of this manure that is available at CDR.

A side note to the topic "donkey droppings":
Donkey droppings are appreciated as one of the best natural manures. If donkeys have mainly been fed with hay, straw, grass and wood, their droppings have a very low content of nitrogen so that plants manured with the droppings do not get burnt. This manure is ideal for berry bushes and roses, but it is also excellent for the rest of the garden.

Dog dirt is picked up every day, too, but separately, since the dirt must be disposed of.

Picking up donkey droppings all over the area

Hoove and pelage care

Scratching out the hooves is quite important. Dirt and stones are removed from the hooves by means of a hoove pick. Stones in the hooves usually cause pain when the donkey walks.

A CDR animal care worker showed me the technique of removing dirt and stones from the hooves. Since I already had a lot of experience, I could start immediately.

Donkeys enjoy the brushing of their pelage which promotes the change of coat. As soon as a donkey has been brushed, another one will appear immediately and try to draw the attention to himself by nudging the workers with his head.

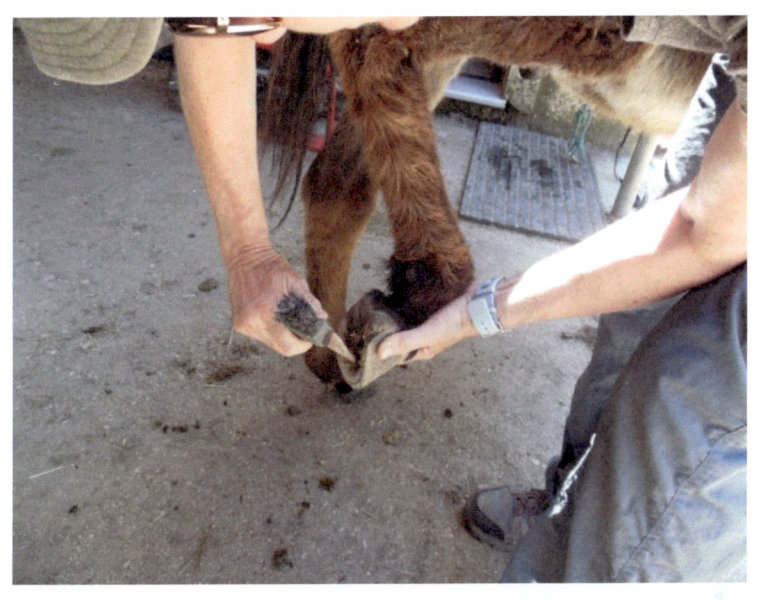

Body care

Donkeys with bare spots on their skin need sun protection. For this purpose natural loam is applied to the bare spots with a brush.

The eyes of a donkey need care as well. The eye rims are cleaned with a special cosmetic wet wipe.

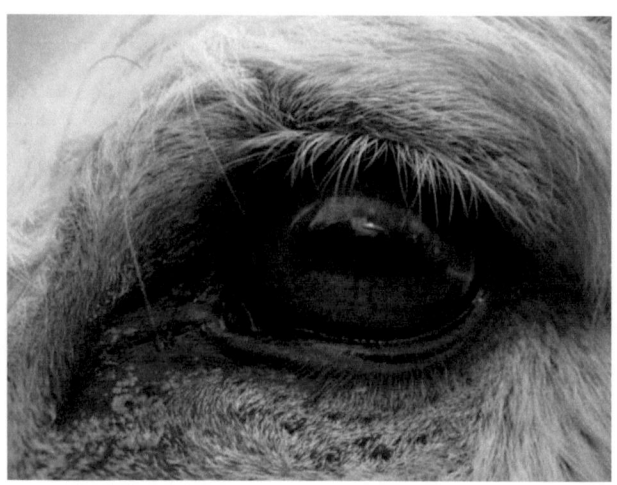

Applying natural loam to the bare spots as a sunscreen

Cleaning the eye rims

Feeling fine!

Donkeys are bon vivants - they love massages and keep their feet still in a devout manner.

There are many acupressure points on their ears having effects on other parts of the body. Stimulating these points has a positive effect to the immune system. Pressing the points at the ear nipple base has an effect on the meridian influencing the digestive and respiratory system.

When massaging the donkey, the forefinger and the middle finger are wandering over the body with a slight pressure, the thumb is only dragged behind and the donkey can relax.

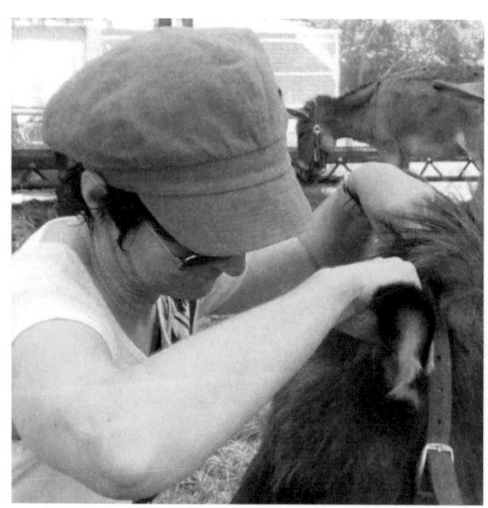

Dina, a blind female donkey, is extremely fond of getting massages. She is one of my adopted donkeys. On the last day of my stay I told her good-bye in my way: Massaging her for half an hour before the feeding in the evening. Actually I had not planned to return to her since farewells are so hard. However, I had not expected that Dina's hearing is so good.

A German tourist couple had arrived that I guided through the donkey station. Dina was at the other end of the area where the blind donkeys usually are and I was standing in front of the area together with the visitors, telling them about my experiences with donkeys. Dina heard my voice, put up her ears, marched towards me using my voice as an orientation help and stopped in front of me.

The blind donkeys know their area well and enjoy moving there freely.

Guided tours

Another task is showing the donkey shelter to visitors. Visitors may tour around there free of charge every day from 10 a.m. until 5 p.m.

The visitors are shown the complete area and they are informed on the tasks and aims of CDR. It is important that visitors get information on donkeys to know what is good for them or bad. The more people are informed on keeping donkeys, how to treat them correctly, what they need, what should strictly be avoided, and pass on this knowledge to as many people as possible, the better the lives of donkeys will be.

The visitors may brush the donkeys or walk around with them so that they come to know these lovable animals better and better.

Visitors brushing donkeys...

...or going for a walk with them

Horses

Principally, CDR does not adopt any horses, but when seeing this pony in August 2012 it was impossible to say "no". Elafri recovered very well after five months of nursing her back to health.

 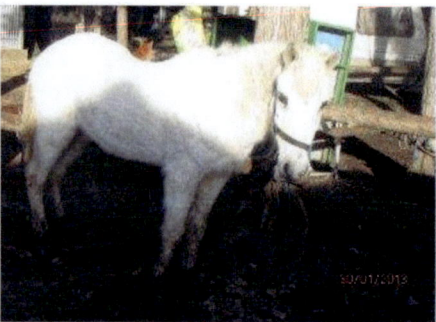

The daily working routine with ponies includes feeding, body care, bringing the ponies to the meadow, exchanging water and cleaning the stables.

On the way to the meadow

Dogs

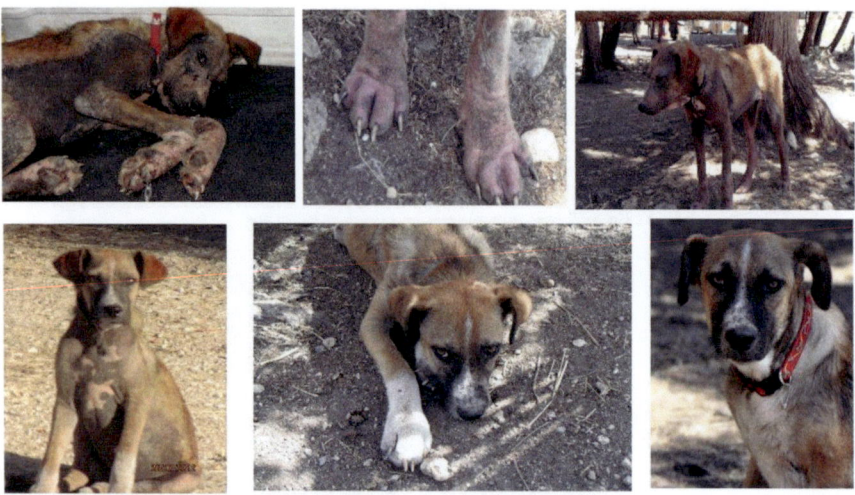

Dogs are not part of CDR's rescue program either. Two examples show the valuable work CDR also does for "unwelcome" dogs. In both cases a picture of misery recovered to be a fine specimen of a dog.

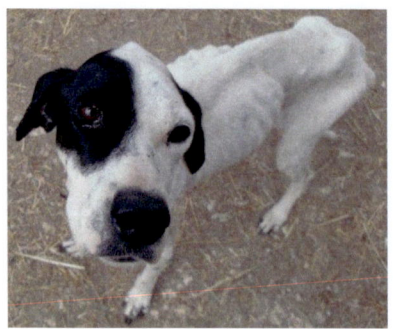  

The daily working routine for the dogs includes feeding, administering medicine as required, picking up dog dirt, walking and giving them a lot of tender loving care.

Puppies

Moments of happiness

This was one of my most beautiful moments at CDR:
An animal lover from Germany gave this puppy a new home.

Small animals

I had to care for

- two rabbits
- one hen
- one turkey
- and two cats

living in an enclosure for small animals. The cats can get out through an exit for cats and love spending time on the meshed roof. They enjoy lying on it like in a hammock.

In the enclosure for animals feeding is done in the morning and in the evening, the water is changed and the enclosure is cleaned by means of a rake. When the roofs of the four animal houses are dirty, they are cleaned with water and with a brush.

Additionally to their fodder the rabbits get grass, dandelions and blooms that were picked while walking the dogs.

Finally the egg(s) the hen might have laid, is (are) collected.

The hen loves cuddling up to the turkey while sleeping. It is so nice to see that the rabbits, the hen, the turkey and the cats live in such harmony.

Cats

Cats enjoy their freedom in the donkey shelter at CDR, but they always return to their regular places after touring around. These places are in the enclosure for small animals, in the kitchen for animals and in a caravan.

The cats are fed twice a day and get fresh water.

I was also responsible for a cat feeding station in front of the access to CDR that had been established for cats that did not want to enter the CDR area. One of these cats loves sitting on a tree next by the entrance. She welcomed me every morning by miaowing, however, she never went on the area. She gets her fodder from said feeding station.

Cats always find the strangest places for having a rest. They come regularly in the break periods and sit down next to or on the workers waiting for tender loving care.

No break without animals ☺

Harmony and sympathy among the animals

Here donkeys, horses, dogs and cats live together in harmony. Moreover they even feel sympathy for another animal not feeling well. It seems that the dogs and cats "feel responsible" for the donkeys. In most cases, a dog or a cat is near an ill or injured donkey.

In this picture you see Schmoo sitting in the box of an injured donkey after his arrival at CDR.

This cat was keeping watch over an ill donkey

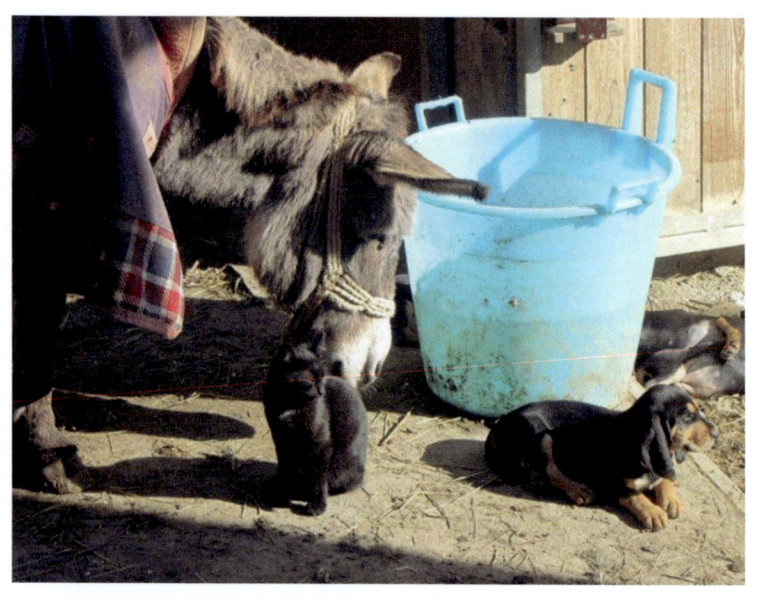

Patiently the donkey let the puppies play around

Cuddly donkey backs

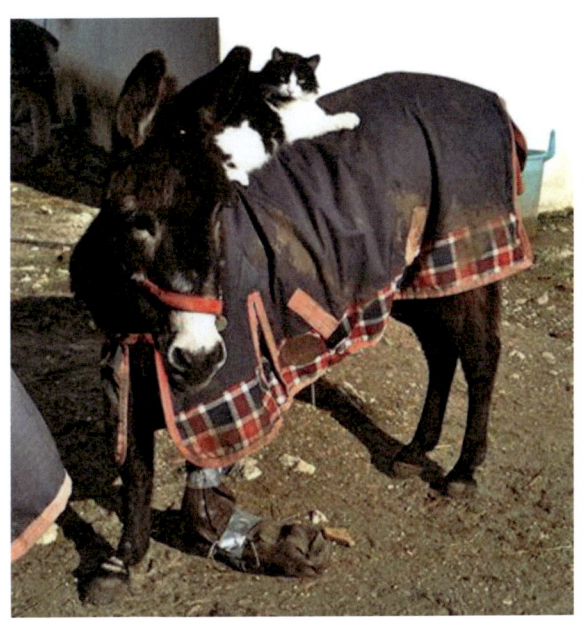

Teamwork

CDR animal care workers, voluntary helpers from Greece and voluntary helpers from various countries. Various nations having different mentalities encounter here, but they have one thing in common: **They love animals and they want to help them.**

They always work together hand in hand and knowledge is passed on from one volunteer to another in order to support the CDR animal care workers in the job training of new helpers.

Conclusion

At the entrance of the treatment stable there is a plain DIN A 4 sheet showing the following citation:

We can do no great things, only small things with great love
Mother Teresa

This citation describes exactly the working manner and way of thinking of CDR. CDR does not have much money, but they give the animals a lot of love. The main focus is on the well-being of the animals. In these two weeks I was working in all animal areas (small animals, horses, dogs, cats and donkeys) and I was deeply impressed how much love can be seen in the animal care.

Visitors I guided through the donkey station always admired the high quality of work that is done here.

I have been convinced by the work at CDR. Although I flew back with sad feelings since the fortnight had passed so quickly, there was a good feeling knowing that CDR does all for the animals they can.

It is true: Whoever has come here will return. I have already booked "my" two weeks next year. This time in February to experience work and conditions in the winter.

I can recommend everybody who wants to engage in animal welfare to "donate" a part of the annual leave and to actively work at CDR to see all what is possible.

Not everybody has the possibility to "donate" two weeks of his or her annual leave. In any case I would recommend to visit CDR during holidays on Corfu to have a look at the donkey shelter. The way to the stabling complex branches off the main street between Corfu City and Paleokastritsa. From here just follow the information signs.

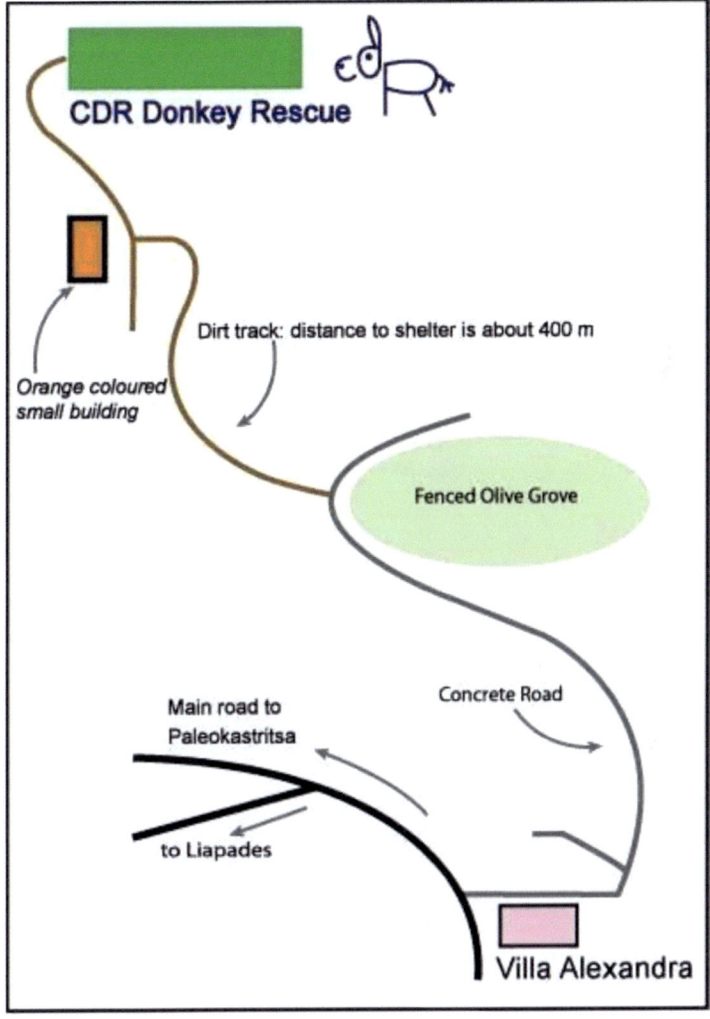

Adoption of a donkey

Adopting a donkey offers the possibility to help all other donkeys in the station as well. You will have a more personal contact to the donkey you have chosen, you will get an adoption document and newsletters (in different languages) informing on how the donkey gets along.

The annual costs are 90 Euros or 76 GBP Sterling.

More information on adoption (payment, bank details etc.) you will find on the homepage **www.corfu-donkeys.com**

Of course the most attractive way is to choose "his" or "her" own donkey at CDR. On the next pages I would like to present some of the approximately 60 donkeys:

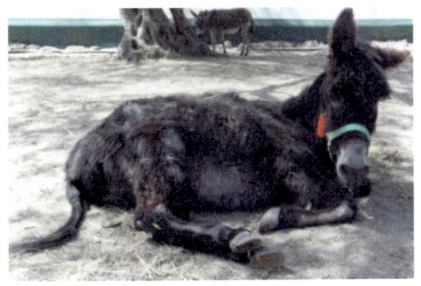

Calimero

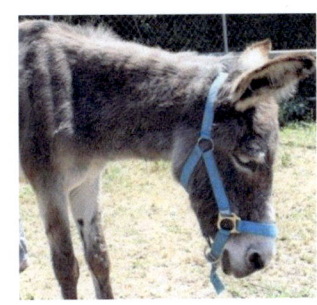

Dina

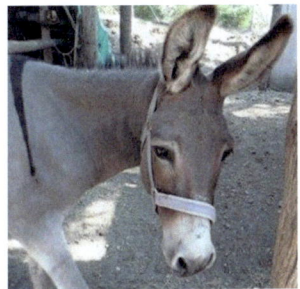

Ciglia

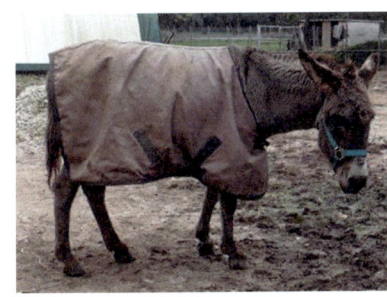

Hancy

Cookie

Amalia

65

Irithia

Kaluha

Tequilla

Tonika

Artemis

Kithi

Lente

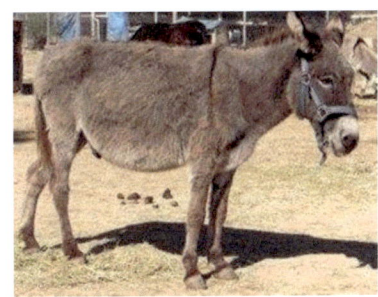

Titch

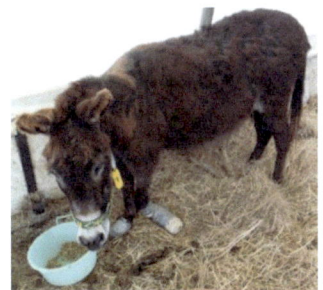

Xara

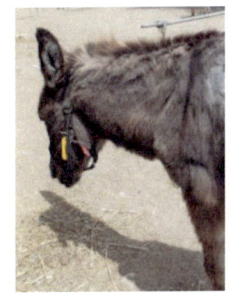

Zante

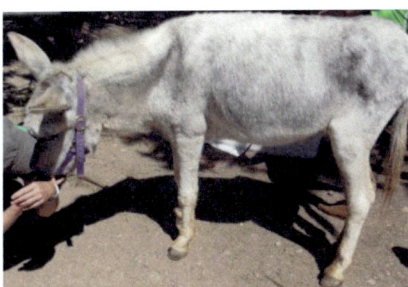

Zachari alias „Zac"

How to support CDR?

Any donation, no matter how small, makes a huge difference to the donkeys of Corfu.

For payments in **Germany** please use:

Sparkasse Berchtesgadener Land
Name: Dagmar Lohrenz
IBAN DE79710500000020140877
BIC/SWIFT BYLADEM1BGL
Verwendungszweck: Spende CDR

For payment in **UK** please use

Lloyds Bank
Name: Friends of Corfu Donkey Rescue
BIC LOYDGB21368
A/C No: 01308617
Sort Code: 30-90-99

If you require a German receipt for tax purposes (50 € or above only please) send to the account below and give your full name and address (for payments made so far and new ones)

Martina und Jürgen Bolz Stiftung
IBAN DE58500700100700780000
BiC/SWIFT-Code DEUTDEFFXXX
Verwendungszweck: Spende CDR

For donation of **other countries** our Greek bank details are:

Alpha Bank
Account Name: Kerkyraiki Diasosi Onon
IBAN: GR94 0140 6800 6800 0210 1311 223
SWIFT CRBAGRAA
Donation CDR

More information about CDR

Homepage of CDR:
www.corfu-donkeys.com

Contact information:
Judy Quinn
(0030)6947 375 992
Email: corfudonkey@gmail.com

Facebook
English FB-Group: Corfu Donkey Rescue
German FB-Group: Corfu Donkey Rescue (deutsch)

The profit earned by selling the following books will also go to Corfu Donkey Rescue:

FUZZY – the story of a Greek donkey

The first 10years of
CORFU DONKEY RESCUE